The Bubble Collector

poems and drawings
Vikram Madan

Praise for 'The Bubble Collector':

"I read this **lively and kid-friendly collection** with much merriment."
- *J. Patrick Lewis*, *U.S. Children's Poet Laureate (2011-2013) and author of over 75 children's poetry books*

"Vikram Madan's **The Bubble Collector** will have you **bubbling over with laughs**. This light and lithe collection has dozens of poems and drawings that will **surely tickle your funny bone**."
- *Douglas Florian*, *creator of many acclaimed and award-winning poetry books including Dinothesaurus, Insectlopedia and Shiver Me Timbers!*

"**The Bubble Collector** is **a witty look at the world** through the poems and drawings of Vikram Madan. Kids and adults will identify again and again with such predicaments as "Unkempt" (putting off getting a haircut), "Detention" (saying the wrong thing at the wrong time to the wrong person), "Impatient", "All Steamed Up!!!" and page after page of others. **Get a copy. Sit back and enjoy!**"
- *David L. Harrison*, *award-winning author of over 80 poetry, fiction and non-fiction books (with over 15 million copies sold world-wide).*

"It is evident how **much love and time** went into the production of this book"
- *Lee Bennett Hopkins*, *The Pied Piper of Poetry, Anthologist for 113 Children's Poetry Anthologies (a world record!)*

The Bubble Collector: Poems and Drawings by Vikram Madan

Copyright © 2013 Vikram Madan

Madan, Vikram
  The Bubble Collector: Poems and Drawings / Vikram Madan
Includes index.
  ISBN 978-1482397611
  1. Children's poetry, American. 2. Humorous poetry, American. 3. American Poetry. 4. Humorous Poetry

Book Design by Vikram Madan.
No cartoon characters were harmed in the making of this book.

DEDICATED TO MY FAMILY
AND TO EVERYONE WHO
LOVES BOOKS

Acknowledgements

My heartfelt appreciation to Jack Prelutsky, J. Patrick Lewis, David L. Harrison, Douglas Florian, and Lee Bennett Hopkins for their kind support and encouragement related to the writing of humorous poetry. Thanks to Alisha Dall'osto for reading the manuscript and suggesting the title for this book. Another thanks to David L. Harrison for his poetry-centric blog without which the poems *'Ominous Sign'*, *'Ogre's Meal'*, and *'Midnight Hour'* would not have existed at all. Thanks to Renée LaTulippe for the blog post that inspired the poem *'All Steamed Up!!!'*. A tip o' the hat to Shel Silverstein for his inspirational body of work. And last, but not the least, this work would not have been possible without the support of my family (Madhu, Jawahar, and Jahnvi), whose patience and understanding allowed me to spend the hundreds and hundreds of hours it took to create this book.

The Bubble Collector

WELCOME

Welcome you who enter here
Come step right up and *lend* an ear
And in return, for just a while
I promise you shall laugh and smile

What's that? You say you've changed your mind?
You want your ear back? How unkind!
Alas, you may not claim that ear -
You should have read the small print here[*]

Your ear is now part of this book
Well, turn the page and take a look...

---

[*]By reading this here poem, any ear loaned in part or whole, is henceforth considered permanently loaned to this book and you and your siblings, parents, cousins, classmates, friends, enemies, frenemies, teachers, pets, evil twins and imaginary friends hereby agree to forever waive all claims whatsoever for the return of such ear.

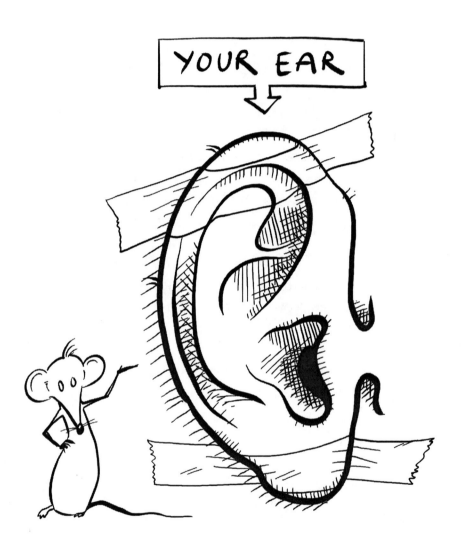

PERFECT PET

You find turtles are snappy
You fear that dogs have fleas
And snakes give you the willies
And hamsters make you sneeze

You said no to iguanas
Rejected raising rats
You nixed lizards and geckos
And vetoed getting cats

You say birds are too messy
And rabbits multiply
Tarantulas are creepy
And ferrets run awry

You disapprove of gerbils
And toads and hermit crabs
You fret about diseases
And lice and tics and scabs

So I did much researching
For pets you won't regret
And I think you will concur
I've found the perfect pet!

COME ON IN, THE WATER'S LOVELY

Come on in, the water's lovely
You and I can take a swim
We can wade or we can waddle
Cannonball, if that's your whim

We can scuba, dive and snorkel
We can float or we can sink
We'll be joined by one or two friends
More is merry, don't you think?

BUDDING ARTIST

I love to paint animals
I can paint them night and day
I love to paint animals...

...But they always run away.

THE GOURMET

If you'd like to feed me dinner
I won't grumble, gripe or bawl
Serve me any taste or texture
I will gladly eat it all

Bittermelon, Arugula
Kielbasa or Cassoulet
Polenta or Manicotti
Frittata or Squid Fillet

Tofu, Tempeh, Grits, and Seaweed
Kim Chi, Collard Greens, and Beets
Liver, Haggis, Curdled Yogurt
Wasabi on Pickled Meats

Make it bland or make it spicy
Make it big or make it small...

...Long as I can add my ketchup
I will gladly eat it all!

THE THING

It's awful and appalling and
  It's yuckier than yuck
It's hideous and horrendous and
  It's nasty, run amuck

It's dreadful and disgusting and
  It's loathsome and so coarse
The sight of it is certain to
  Inspire much remorse

It's rancid and repulsive and
  Sure to make you vomit
I guess I should have noticed it...

...Before I stepped upon it.

CURSE OF THE CATCHY TUNE

A catchy tune I heard last June
That scintillating, snappy tune
Is still cavorting round and round
  And round inside my head…

The melody's unsinkable
It turns my thoughts unthinkable
Echo-cho-choing all around
  Unbound inside my head…

I hear it when I'm waking up
And through the day, and when I sup
And I go to bed with that sound
  Rebounding in my head...

It's been this way for half a year
The tune's the only thing I hear
The harmony hopelessly wound
  Around my aching head...

A gypsy said, to break this curse
I need to write a little verse
A poem to which shall be bound
  The sound inside my head...

And when another hears that rhyme
The tune shall leave my haunted mind
And go propound, perplex, astound
  Confound some other's head...

You've read this poem? Hooray! I'm free!
Now soon *you'll* hear that melody
That tune profound that shall surround
  And hound *your* little head.

FRANKEN-JACK AND FRANKEN-JILL

Franken-Jack and Franken-Jill
Lurching, lurching up the hill
Testing out the new physiques
Doctor Stein has built this week

"Buck-Et-Take-Up!", F-Jack groans
"Wa-Ter-Bring-Down!", F-Jill moans
Fill the bucket at the top
Careful not to slop a drop

Franken-Jill and Franken-Jack
Heaving, swaying, stagger back
Teeter, totter, two left feet
Trip and tumble to the street

Franken-Jill's the first to rise
Dusts her dress, adjusts her eyes
Looks at Franken-Jack and frowns
"Frank-En-Jack,-You-Big-Hurt-Crown!"

Franken-Jack gets up and looms
Feels his head, then rages, fumes
"Think-Me-Head-Doc-No-Good-Bind!
Lost-Me-Now-Me-Piece-Of-Mind!"

ALL STEAMED UP!!!

I'm steamed up and I'm ruffled!
My blood is boiling hot!
I'm flying off the handle!
Erupting on the spot!

I'm ranting and I'm foaming!
I'm seeing red and black!
I've blown a fuse and gasket,
And every kind of stack!

It's hot under my collar!
The sticks are in my craw!
I'm having a conniption!
I'm ticked off to a flaw!

I'm going off the deep end!
I'm going through the roof!
I'm going on the warpath!
I'm upset at your goof!

Your blunder is colossal!
I'm calling the police!
You put my piece of dessert
On top of –(gasp!)– my veggies!

IMPATIENT

I find it very, very hard to .... wait
I'm always number one out of the .... gate
I sneak a peek when told I should not .... look
I skip ahead and read the end of .... books
I open Christmas presents back in .... June
I often blurt out secrets way too .... soon
They call me hasty, impatient, and .... keen
That's how I am and that is how I've .... been
But there's a lesson in this tummy .... ache:
I'm never eating cakes before they're .... baked.

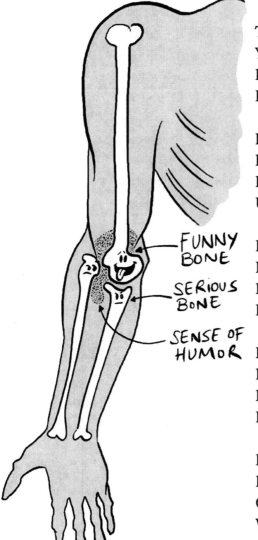

FUNNY BONE

SERIOUS BONE

SENSE OF HUMOR

LOST: ONE SENSE OF HUMOR

The tale is spreading quickly;
You must have heard the rumor
I hurt my funny bone and then
I lost my sense of humor

I've looked for it all summer
I've searched afar and near
I'm feeling very dismal and
Unsmilingly severe

Hilarity eludes me
My wit induces tears
My jokes are flat as pancakes and
Repulsive to all ears

My puns are vile and pun-gent
My tales of jest appall
My gags induce much gagging and
My banter makes them bawl

Don't let this happen to you
Protect your funny bone
Or else you too might write a poem
Whose ending is a 'groan'.

GORGEOUS HAIR

The secret to my gorgeous hair
Is hours and hours of daily care
I shampoo it and rinse it thrice
(I use six kinds to make it nice)
I follow this with spray and gel
And hair tonic (massaged in well)
And brushes for the curls and knots
And flat irons to straighten spots
My fifty combs ensure its state
Is tidy and immaculate
I keep it out of sun and rain
And when I'm done... I start again
Oh yes, it takes a lot of care
To look after my gorgeous hair

MATHLETE

Oh, soon I'll conquer *Algebra*
Do *Geometry* for keeps
Trigonometry's trivia
I'll master in my sleep

Quadratics and *Factorials*
Will be my second skin
And *Calculus's* conundrums
I'll take out for a spin

Differentials and *Vectors*
I'll *Integrate* with ease
Eat *Minimas* and *Maximas*
For breakfast when I please

Logarithms and *Matrices*
I'll entertain for jest
But first I've got to overcome
This mystifying test!

THE PROMISE

Dear Dad, you made a promise
But we know you forgot
A treasure hunt is what you said
So now that's what you've got

This time *we* did the burying
And made the cryptic map
This time *you'll* do the finding
(After you've had your nap)

The hunt will be exciting
So won't you join us please?
Our treasure chest contains, you see
Your wallet, phone and keys!

SOUND EFFECTS

Sloshing water (in my bottle)
Chewing loudly (on my gum)
Hiccupping (by faking hiccups)
Humming songs (that no one hums)
Armpit music (made with armpits)
Sound Effects! (Toot! Honk! Whirr! Hiss!)
Long drives can be, oh, so boring
Need more sounds for bugging Sis!

A DRAGON TAIL

I caught a Dragon by the tail
But wasn't holding tight
It took off in a puff of smoke
And left me feeling fright
And slipped out of my sweaty hands
And vanished in the night

The next day I put on thick gloves
And vowed to hold on firm
But I did not anticipate
How well Dragons can squirm
Once more it left me standing there
(Alone with all my germs)

And that's why I used super-glue
The finest I could find
And six weeks later I can vouch,
How well that glue did bind!
Wherever now the Dragon flies,
I follow close behind...

RUBBER DUCK

A showdown with my rubber duck:
Hey Duck, I said, *You're out of luck!*
This bathtub just ain't big enough
  For use by both of us

A kid like me, I need my space
A duck like you is out of place
You're yellow, small, and not so tough
  So leave without a fuss

Yes, long ago you were my friend
But all good things must reach an end
Now you must go so please don't cry
  Or squeak your squeaky squeaks!

But, oh, that duck had lots of pluck
He called my bluff and now I'm stuck
He threw *me* out and that is why...

...I haven't bathed in weeks.

LIMERICKS FROM THE LUNCH ROOM

Said a dainty first grader named Mabel,
As she licked her food right off the table,
  "Each lick that I sneak
  Has a flavor unique -
So I'll do this as long as I'm able!"

There was a third grader named José
Who blew bubbled milk through his nose-ay
  When the milk bubbles spewed
  The girls all "Eeeew" "Eeeeew"-ed
While the boys all thought it was grandiose-ay

There was a fifth grader named Nelly
Whose lunches were terribly smelly
  She'd gobble them quick
  Saying "That does the trick -
Can't smell it once it's in my belly!"

WHO'S GOT TIME

Who's got time for making beds
And picking stuff that's on the floor?
Who's got time for walking dogs
Or getting something from the store?
Rinsing dishes? Folding clothes?
Emptying garbage? No, Señor!
What we're doing's more important
Who's got time for doing chores?

DAD'S DINNER SPECIAL

Our dad loves making meatloaf
He makes it with much pride
The more he beams the more we fret
About what lurks inside

He prefers strange ingredients
Quinoa, Tofu, Beans
Kohlrabi, Bok Choy, Leeks, and Chard
And Spinach, Kale, and Greens

Zucchini, Beets and Pumpkins
Radish And Sprouts and Stew
And all of this week's leftovers
Are dawdling in there too

And when that meatloaf's finished
It's something we must eat
It wouldn't be so bad if he'd
Sometimes include some meat.

CHEETAH

The Cheetah's very fleet-ah
On its four swift feet-ah
If you see one in the street-ah
Don't end up as its meat-ah

GIRAFFES

With awkward legs,
and necks too long,
Proportions that look
somewhat wrong,
Each time they walk,
it seems to all,
They're headed for
a clumsy fall.

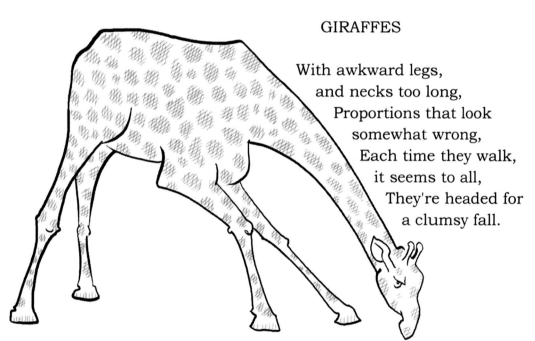

SLUG

The word that best
describes a slug
Is ugh!

TALK LIKE A PIRATE

AVAST, ME HEARTIES!
AAAAAAR! (Said I)
WALK THAT PLANK YE BILGE RAT!
AYE! AYE!

It was International-Talk-Like-a-Pirate-Day[*]
I was saying all the things that pirates would say
I was bold, I was brash, I was brazen and loud
Me swagger was makin' me mateys all proud

YE SCURVY LANDLUBBER!
YE MANGY OLD WRECK!
YE BETTER STOP YAPPIN'!
START SWABBIN' THE DECK!

I was doing it so well that I have to confess
I forgot that this wasn't how one should address
A School Principal.

---

[*] Every Year on September 19th

32

AWFUL

I think it's rather awful
How much flies love my waffle
They're buzzing and they're hopping
And they're eating all my toppings

UNKEMPT

Yes I said I'll get a haircut
Not today – it'll have to wait
Maybe we can try in Autumn
After all the birds migrate

unBIRTHDAY

Today is my unbirthday
It's your unbirthday too
Let's unexchange unpresents
Unhave an un-to-do

We'll unthrow an unparty
We'll unbake an uncake
We'll uninflate unballoons
Unclowns? No unmistake!

Unsmashing unpiñatas
Unrelishing untricks
Unordering unpizzas
Unwatching some unflicks

And when tomorrow turns up
We'll unstart un-anew
Tomorrow's my unbirthday
It's your unbirthday too!

HAPPY UNBiRTHDAY!! YAY!

No! UNHAPPY UNBiRTHDAY!! UNYAY!!

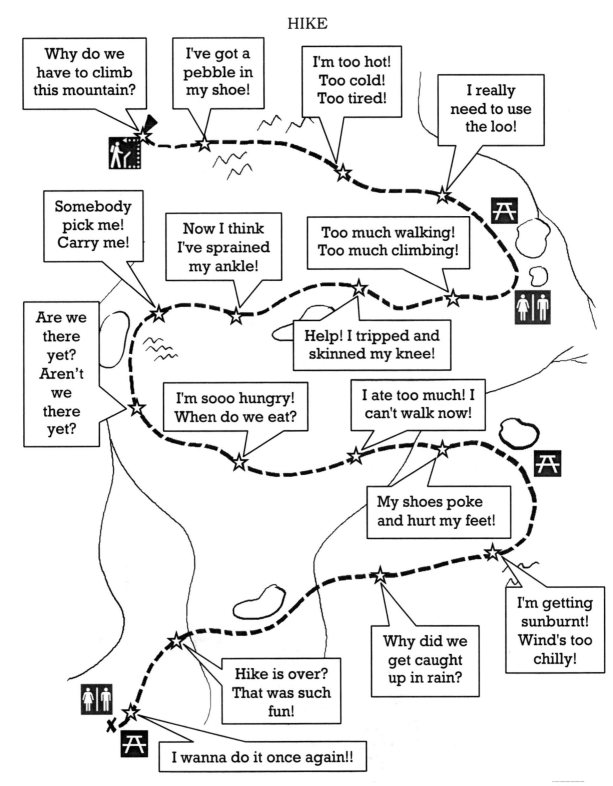

GECKO

The Gecko does it's wheeling-dealing ...
On the walls and on the ceiling ...
Should it slip and fall down reeling ...
What's left won't be too appealing ...

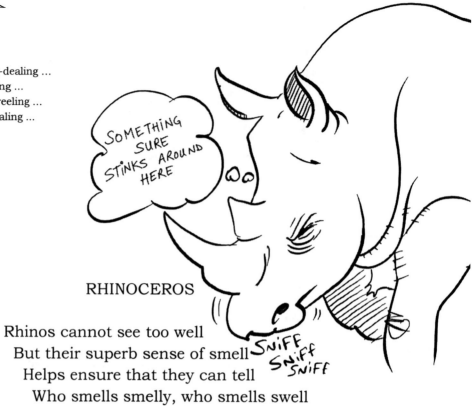

RHINOCEROS

Rhinos cannot see too well
But their superb sense of smell
Helps ensure that they can tell
Who smells smelly, who smells swell

OSTRICH

From *weight of wing* to *stretch of leg*
From *reach of neck* to *size of egg*
All Ostrich parts are huge in size
Except ... that one between its eyes.

YOGA

Our mums make us do yoga
They say it'll help us grow-ga
We wear our little toga
And quietly tiptoe-ga
We breathe in deep and slow-ga
And stretch our bodies so-ga
We bend and twist and flow-ga
And when it's time to go-ga
Please unknot us, you know-ga?

HAND-ME-DOWN

Hand-me-down shoes
Hand-me-down pants
Hand-me-down socks from me
Hand-me-down Aunts
Hand-me-down shirt
With a hand-me-down flair
No one better hand-me-down
Underwear!

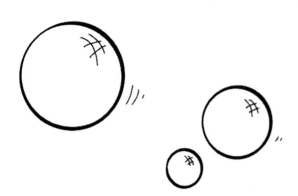

THE BUBBLE COLLECTOR

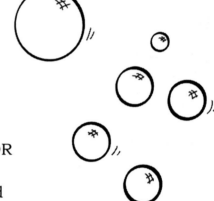

Well ever since I was a kid
I've dreamed of catching bubbles
And so I chase them endlessly
Through all my joys and troubles

But catching them is, I have found,
Harder than it appears
Each time I get my hands on one
It *always* disappears!

Now some might be dejected by
How bubbles vanish so
But me? I'm not the quitting kind
So off again I go...

IN THE BACK OF THE 'FRIDGERATOR
A Love Story

Really Old met Really Stale
In the back of the 'fridgerator
"Love at First Smell!" they declared;
Each vowed its love was greater

"You and I shall have much fun-gus!"
"Let's grow m-old together!"
And thus they lived in putrid bliss
And rotted with each other

One sudden day, a hand reached in
And decomposed the pair
And one was left mourning the loss
Of one no longer there

Now would this tale have tragic end,
As one languished and yearned?
Not yet – the ordeal continued –
Mum's cleansing hand returned!

Before too long the fridge was bare
And scrubbed from well within
And the lovers? Reunited!
In the heart of the compost bin.

RAINING PART I

It's Raining and
It's Raining and
It's Raining
Raining
Raining
And –
Whatever
made you
think
that I'm
complaining???

RAINING PART II

Idt's rainig and idt's rainig and idt's
Rainig Rainig Rainig
I godt pretty soakig wedt and my
Nodse isndt dranig
And I'm running just a fever and
The chillds have me strainig
And thdis time...
I readlly am complainig!

BANANAS

Bananas! Bananas!
I love to smell and peel them!
Bananas! Bananas!
I love to squish and feel them!
Bananas! Bananas!
I love to chop and mash them!
Bananas! Bananas!
I love to hide and stash them!
Bananas! Bananas!
I love to meet and greet them!
Bananas! Bananas!
I just don't love to eat them!

I POKED A CYCLOPS IN THE EYE

I poked a Cyclops in the eye
But I should not have done that
He swatted me into the sky
But he should not have done that

I kicked him on his massive shin
But I should not have done that
He dropped me in the garbage bin
But he should not have done that

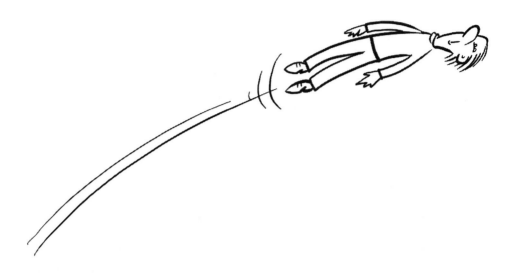

I pinched his cheek until it hurt
But I should not have done that
He ripped the buttons off my shirt
But he should not have done that

I glued his hair into a bunch
But I should not have done that
He ate up all my books for lunch
But he should not have done that

And so, for breaking every rule,
We have to stay back after school
Perhaps some other place or time
We shall once more revive our duel

PRISONER

Tick, tick, tick, tick,
Tick, tick, tick, tick,
Tick, tick, tick, tick,
Tick, tick, tock
I'm a captive, I'm a hostage
I'm a prisoner of that clock

From the morning till the evening
How that clock controls my fate
Time to do this! Time to do that!
Hurry up! Hurry up! You'll be late!

Always rushing here and there and
Always running to some place
I can't dawdle, I can't linger
I can't do things at my pace

Day's-a-passing! Breath's-a-wasting!
Things need doing! Clocks will chime
How I wish there was a world in
Which we kept no track of time

(Except, of course, when I'm
  stuck in Math class).

HOLES

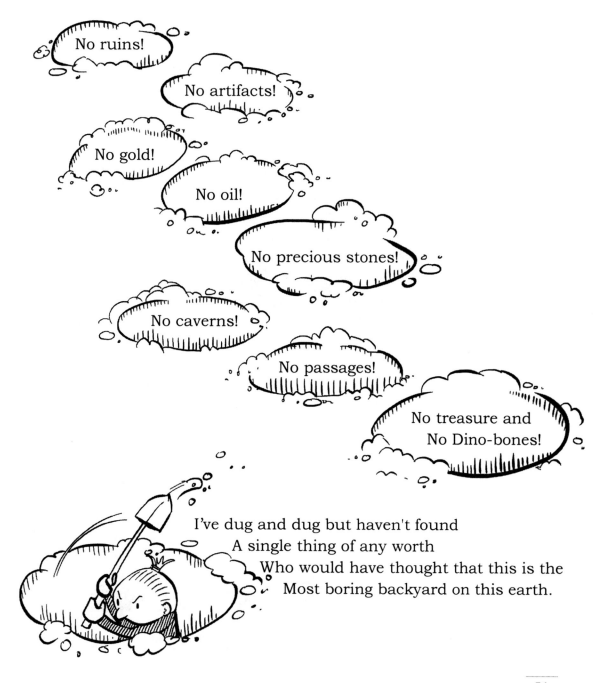

I've dug and dug but haven't found
A single thing of any worth
Who would have thought that this is the
Most boring backyard on this earth.

BALLRUS

Never, never bounce the Ballrus
(Though it bounces rather well)
For a bouncy bouncing Ballrus
Can be very hard to quell

It will bounce off every wall of
Every room inside your house
It will flatten all your stuff and
It won't spare your cat or mouse

It will bounce out of the window
And go bounding down the street
Crushing all the cars and buses
Squishing anything it meets

It will keep on bouncing, bouncing
(You won't catch it if you run)
So please never bounce the Ballrus
Even though this sounds like fun

SO SLEEPY

Sleepy... so sleepy...
So mind-numbingly sleepy...
...I'm languishing like summer heat
...I've doldrums in my hands and feet
...My arms are brick, my legs are stone
...Don't make me talk, I only moan
...My mind is fogged, my brain is beat
...My every thought is incompl...
...My eyes are grit, my head is sore
...Ignore me if I snort and snore
...I've regressed to a zombie state
...I've lost all care about my fate
...I'm weary in my deepest bone
...My fondest wish? To lie here prone!
...So lead me not to bed or cot
...I want to melt into this spot
...Please let me be and I'll proclaim
...I'll never, ever, ever, never...
Binge all night on video-games.

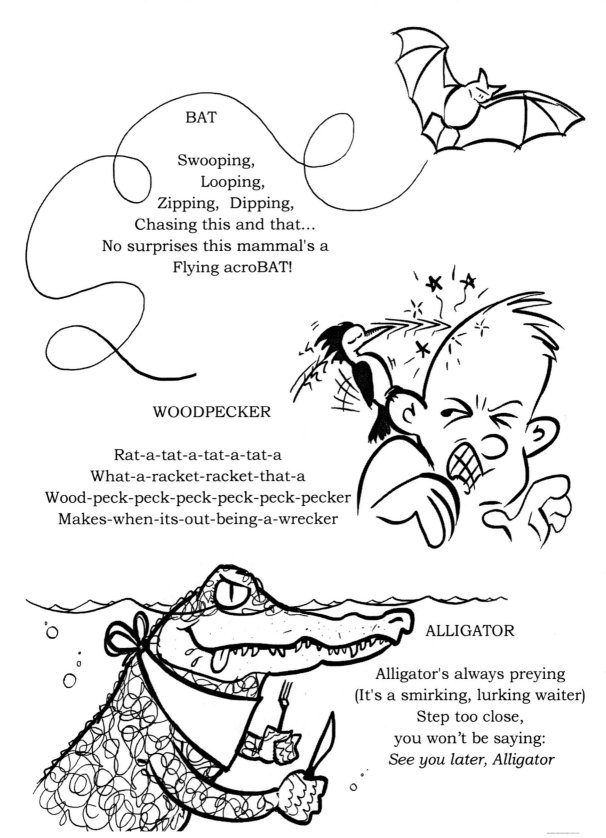

BAT

Swooping,
Looping,
Zipping, Dipping,
Chasing this and that...
No surprises this mammal's a
Flying acroBAT!

WOODPECKER

Rat-a-tat-a-tat-a-tat-a
What-a-racket-racket-that-a
Wood-peck-peck-peck-peck-peck-pecker
Makes-when-its-out-being-a-wrecker

ALLIGATOR

Alligator's always preying
(It's a smirking, lurking waiter)
Step too close,
you won't be saying:
See you later, Alligator

DAREDEVIL

I stood on the beach
At the edge of her reach
And taunted the Sea
To come get me
And what do you know?
— She did :-(

MOVIE NIGHT

It's movie night!
It's movie night!
The popcorn's popped
And gleaming bright
Our blankies snug
Our jammies tight
And everything is groovy!

It's movie night!
It's movie night!
Come settle down
And huddle right
Let's raise the volume,
Dim the lights
Er … did anyone bring a movie?

ABOMINABLY BIG

The Abominable snowman's
    Abominable feet
Left Abominable footprints
    Across our little street

The Abominable tracks are
    Abominably big
They Abominably zag and
    Abominably zig

It's Abominable mission's
Abominably clear
To Abominably instill
Abominable fear

So here we hide and cower
And here we sit and cling
Abominably waiting for
Indomitable Spring.

BREAKFAST

Don't want cornflakes! Don't want porridge!
Don't want eggs or ham!
Don't want pancakes! Don't want bacon!
Don't want links or spam!
Don't want cereal! Don't want french-toast!
Don't want toast or jam!
What I want is very simple
All I want is yams!

I THOUGHT I SAW A DINOSAUR

I thought I saw a Dinosaur
I watched it trundle by
I marveled at its silhouette
Outlined against the sky
But when I moved in closer to
Examine all the fuss
It turned out to be nothing but
A crusty old school bus

I thought I saw a Dinosaur
It paddled in the pond
It bobbed a lanky neck around
Among the lily fronds
But when I moved in closer to
Enjoy its repartee
It turned out to be nothing but
A goose honking at me

I thought I saw a Dinosaur
It chased me down the trail
It sprinted on two lanky limbs
And waved its arms and tail
I tried my best to run away
My efforts were in vain
Mum caught me and scolded me for
Losing my specs again

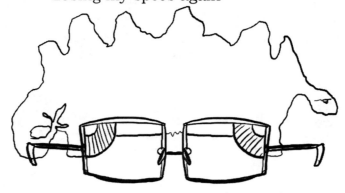

FIFTH GRADE MARCHING BAND

The Fifth Grade Marching Band
Will gladly lend a hand
When someone needs a cheer
The Fifth Grade Band is here

The Fifth Grade Band is loud
We'll gladly rouse the crowd
We'll toot, we'll drum, we'll blow
We'll do it fast and slow

We may not have much skill
But we have lots of will
And one day very soon
We'll learn to play in tune

THINGS I LEARNT
THE HARD WAY

Don't stuff sausage
  in dad's shoe
Don't fix broken
  eggs with glue
Don't hide treasures
  in the waste
Don't brush teeth with
  garlic paste
Don't blow bubbles
  With your nose
Don't eat noodles
  with your toes
Don't wash salad
  with shampoo
Don't paint siblings
  red and blue
Don't drill holes
  in coffee mugs
Don't fill kitchen
  jars with slugs
Don't eat cakes before
  They're baked*
Hope you'll learn from
  my mistakes.

---

* See Page 17

CAMEL

The hump
on the camel's
a bump on the camel
A clump, like a stump,
near the rump of the camel
Should the weight of this hump
cause the camel to slump -
It's the frump of the slump
that makes grumps of the camel

SHARK

Here comes a fin
Slicing the sea
Into portions of
Anxiety

SLINKY

I made a giant slinky toy
I watched it wiggle and twiddle
I pushed it down the stairs and wished
I still wasn't in the middle

TALE OF THE ITCHY WITCH

There was a witch who had an itch
   An itch that waxed and waned
The more she tried to scratch her hide
   The more her itch complained

   The itch *itch-itched*
   The witch *scritch-scritched*
And thus went their refrain
   The more she itched
   The more unhitched
The itchy witch became

With adder's sting and howlet's wing
With eye of newt (or two)
With toe of frog and hair of dog
She brewed a magic brew

She bound this brew of voodoo goo
With all the runes she could
Hoping one drop would surely stop
That pesky itch for good!

With eager lip she took a sip...
It worked without a hitch!
The hex unstitched the vexing twitch
And *vaporized* the itch!

But then the spell nixed *her* as well!
 (It was a *potent* spell!)
So no more itch. And no more witch.
 And no more tale to tell.

The End.

THE THINKER
(OR HOW TO GIVE YOURSELF A HEADACHE)

I know, I think, I know I think,
I know, I think I know,
I know I think I know I think,
I know I think I know

BATHTUB SPIDER

There's a spider in the bathtub
Oh, it gave me such a scare
I was readying for some bathing
When I saw it's eight-eyed stare

Did it fall down from the ceiling?
Did it waft in on the air?
Doesn't matter how it got in
Someone get it out of there

There's a spider in the bathtub
If you peek-in do beware
I suspect that bathtub spider
Isn't wearing underwear

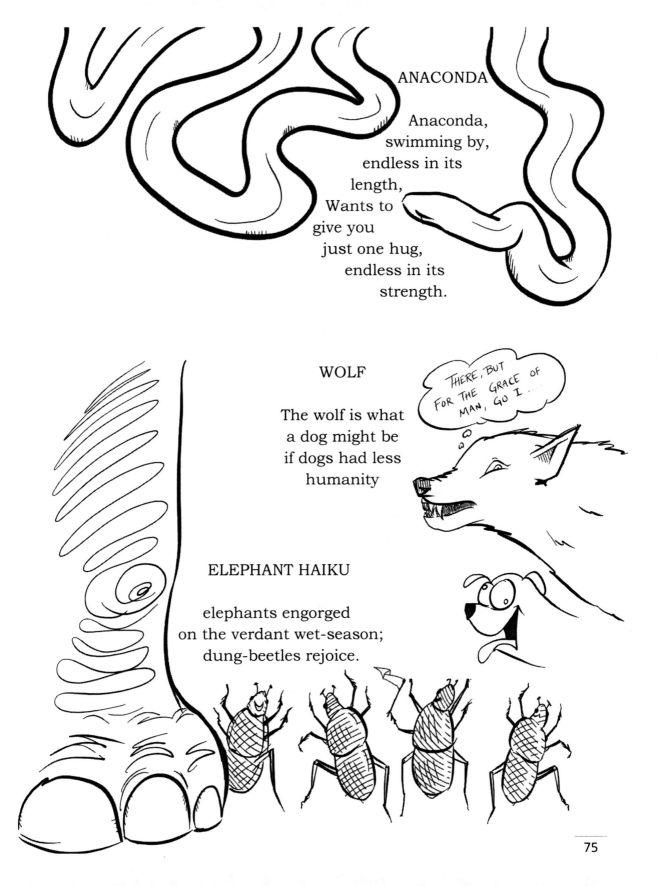

ANACONDA

Anaconda,
swimming by,
endless in its
length,
Wants to
give you
just one hug,
endless in its
strength.

WOLF

The wolf is what
a dog might be
if dogs had less
humanity

THERE, BUT FOR THE GRACE OF MAN, GO I . . .

ELEPHANT HAIKU

elephants engorged
on the verdant wet-season;
dung-beetles rejoice.

PUDDLE-STOMPING

I love to stomp on puddles
I love the splash they make
But not checking the puddle's depth?
That was my big mistake!

BIG BOX STORE CHANT

Can we buy it at your big box store?
At your big box store? At your big box store?
Can we buy it at your big box store?
Of course you can my child!

Can we try it at your big box store?
At your big box store? At your big box store?
Can we try it at your big box store?
Of course you can my child!

Can we fry* it at your -----

NO!

---

* Note: this scene is being enacted by professional cartoon characters. Do NOT try this at home. Or at *any* big box store.

THE YODELER: A BALLAD

Oh, I was born to yodel
And yodeling's what I do
With a Yodel-ay-dee-lay-dee-ay-dee
Yodel-Ay-Dee-Dooo

When the doctor spanked my bottom
I did not cry or coo
Instead I broke out in a song

I never learnt to babble
Gurgle, Ga-Ga, Goo-Goo
The only words I ever said were

In school they'd ask me questions
I never had a clue
The only answer I could give was

If kids would make fun of me
My friends would help me through
I even taught them all to chorus

In town they came to love me
My reputation grew
Soon everyone was joining me in

One day I went on TV
I made them "Aaah!" and "Oooh!"
The ladies, how they swooned when I sang ♫

Now I am rich and famous
My dreams have all come true
The only thing that's left to say is ....

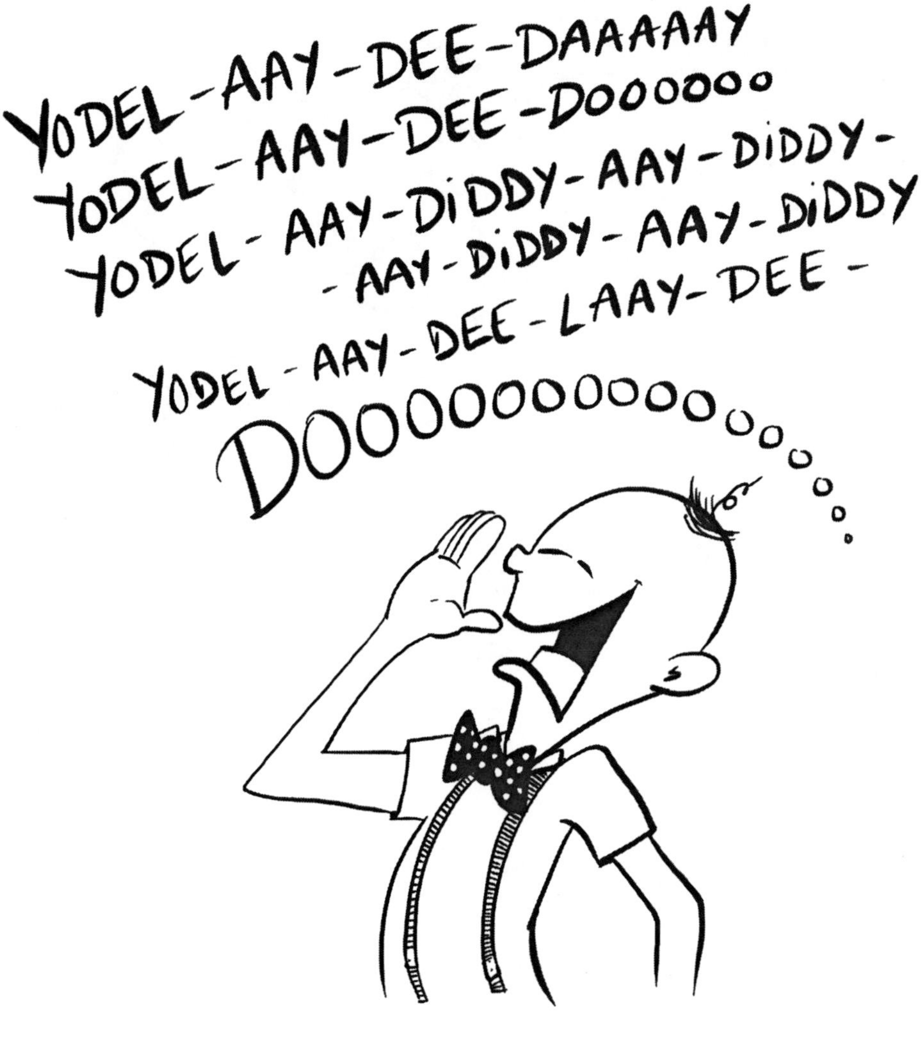

YODEL-AAY-DEE-DAAAAAY
YODEL-AAY-DEE-DOOOOOO
YODEL-AAY-DIDDY-AAY-DIDDY-
-AAY-DIDDY-AAY-DIDDY
YODEL-AAY-DEE-LAAY-DEE-
DOOOOOOOOOOOOOOO

WHAT'S A...

What's a ball...
if not for batting?
What's a pet...
if not for patting?
What's a tree...
if not for climbing?
What's a poem...
if not for rhyming?
What's a song...
if not for singing?
What's a phone...
if not for ringing?
What's a room...
if not for messing?
What's a test*...
if not for guessing?

---

* See Page 21

82

PIGS

They say that pigs are very smart
So I took notes and made a chart
And I can say this much for sure
Their homework skills are very poor

NOT!

The skies are clear
The sun is bright
The Weatherman,
He sure was right!
 (Not!)

STAR LIGHT

Star light, Star bright
First star I see tonight
I wish I may, I wish I might
Really, really draw it right

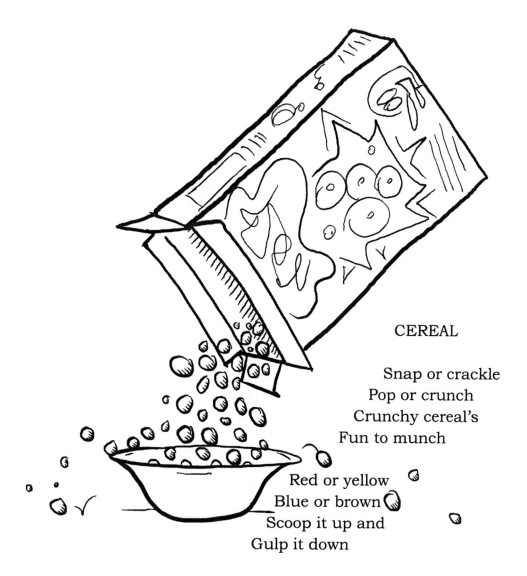

CEREAL

Snap or crackle
Pop or crunch
Crunchy cereal's
Fun to munch

Red or yellow
Blue or brown
Scoop it up and
Gulp it down

Once it's slushy,
Mushy, wet
Feed it quickly
To your pet

DINOSAUR CLOWNS

Yes, Dinosaur Clowns can't act like buffoons
Or make little critters with twisted balloons
They haven't a clue how to strum a guitar
You couldn't squeeze even *one* into a car

Yes, Dinosaur Clowns can't juggle two balls
They can't somersault, do cartwheels or falls
They won't dress in costumes or wear tartan kilts
They can't unicycle or balance on stilts

Yes, Dinosaur Clowns don't paint up their face
They can't skip or run in a three-legged race
They can't ride on zebras or bulls or giraffes
And no one has ever seen one of them laugh

Yes, Dinosaur Clowns can't do magic tricks
But c'mon up folks - get yer tickets here quick!
For even though this is the worst show in town
I'm guessing you've never seen Dinosaur Clowns!

ONE WISH

I don't wish for riches and I don't wish for toys
I don't wish for video games, like the other boys
I don't wish for candy, for chocolates or sweets
I don't wish for pizza or appetizing treats
I don't wish for robots, for aliens or for knights
And freedom from all homework or similar delights
I don't wish for comics, for baseballs or bats
I don't wish my enemies would turn into rats
I have only ONE WISH that I wish I'd get
I wish – *how* I wish – that …

... I had a normal pet!

PIG-EON

That pig-eon on my windowsill
Won't quit making a din
It's keeping me awake instead of
Letting me sleep in

I would not mind if it would coo
Or chirrup, chirp or tweet
A *cheep* or two, a twitter or
A warble would be sweet

But all this creature seems to do
Is snuffle, snort and chew
And why this creature grunts so much
I really wish I knew

It's making a big mess outside
It's been here for a while...

...Should I be glad it's just a pig-
eon, not a crow-codile?

FAIR EXCHANGE

I bith intho an apple
For I love the tasthe of fruith
Now I have a bith of apple
And the apple has my tooth

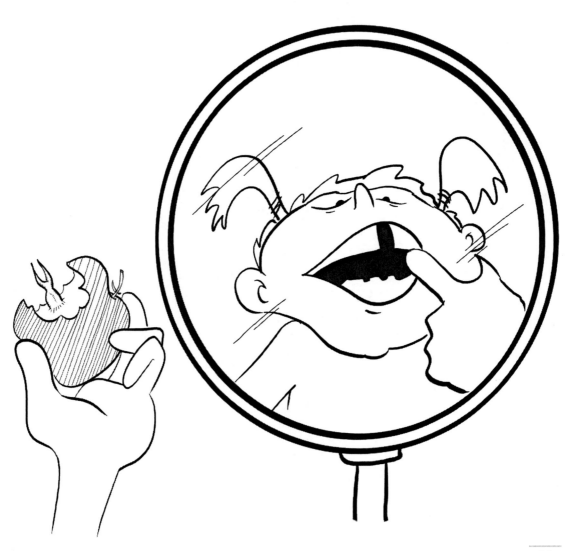

O, VENDING MACHINE!

O, Vending Machine!
We cannot get enough
Of all of your wonderful,
Wonderful stuff

You're loaded with goodies
That we love to eat
They're scrumptious and luscious
And salty and sweet

Your cookies cause cravings
Your wafers are crisp
Your jerky's heavenly
And so are your chips

Your contents we ogle
Your buttons we press
Whatever your prices
We couldn't care less

O, Vending Machine!
How we love you it's true...

...But our parents won't give us
Any money for you. :-(

THE KNIGHT AND THE DRAGON

'You are old,' said the Knight, as he polished his lance
    'And your wings are all tattered and torn
And the ache in your bones surely softens your stance
    And your talons seem dull and well-worn.'

'You are old,' said the Knight, as he mounted his steed
    'And your eyes are beginning to gloss
And the weight of the years surely makes you knock-kneed
    And your scales are all covered with moss.'

'You are old,' said the Knight, as he straightened his shield
    'Do your teeth rattle loose in your gums?
And your blood, once so hot, must lie cold and congealed
    Do you get by on nothing but crumbs?'

'You are old,' said the Knight, as he spurred on his horse
    'And your glory lies faded and maimed
But your fate, though much withered, has shown you remorse
    And left you the keys to my fame!'

'You are old,' said the Knight, as he galloped in fast
    'So why bother to swagger and pose?
As my heart is as kind as my courage is vast
    I shall bring a swift end to your woes.'

'You are old,' said the Knight, as he readied his blow
    'And your breath smells like brimstone and ash
And your fire... still burns?! ... Like a hot... volcano!
    So... hot!!...' And he was gone in a flash.

PARROT

A parrot parrots what you say
A PARROT PARROTS WHAT YOU SAY
A parrot parrots night and day
A PARROT PARROTS WHAT YOU SAY
A parrot's parrots ruin your peace
A PARROT PARROTS WHAT YOU SAY
Unless you make it stop and cease
A PARROT PARROTS WHAT YOU ... SQUAWK*
A ... SQUAWK... PARROTS WHAT YOU ... SQUAWK...
A ... SQUAWK ... SQUAWK... YOU ... SQUAWK...
...SQUA.....
....

A ... SQUAWK ... SQUAWK ...
WHAT YOU ... SQUAWK ...

RATTLESNAKE

You won't hear it hiss or chatter, burble, gibber, prattle
You won't hear much drivel, jabber, babble, blather that'll
Warn you that it's lurking nearby, ready for a battle -
You will know - too late! - you're too close! - when you hear it's rattle!

---

* Note: No animals were harmed in the making of this poem. Do not try this at home.

A PARROT ... SQUAWK ...
SQUAWK... YOU ... SQUAWK ...

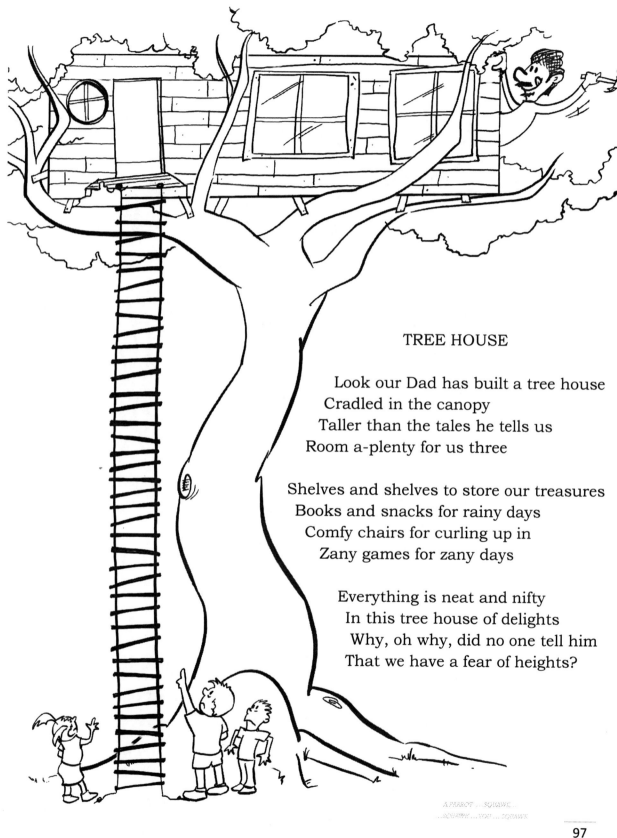

TREE HOUSE

Look our Dad has built a tree house
Cradled in the canopy
Taller than the tales he tells us
Room a-plenty for us three

Shelves and shelves to store our treasures
Books and snacks for rainy days
Comfy chairs for curling up in
Zany games for zany days

Everything is neat and nifty
In this tree house of delights
Why, oh why, did no one tell him
That we have a fear of heights?

A PARROT ... SQUAWK ...
... SQUAWK ... YOU ... SQUAWK

ABRA-CADABRA

"ABRA-CADABRA!"
I will find it
"OPEN-SESAME!"
Have no fear
"HOCUS-POCUS!"
I will find it
Even if it takes all year

"ALLA-KAZIM!"
Somewhere out there
"ALLA-KAZAM!"
Is a spell
Every witch and wizard kid must
"GIL-GIL-GILLI!"
Know it well

It's a spell to turn your dinner
"YUBBA-BUBBA!"
Into treats
No more carrots! No more spinach!
"FLIMFLAM-SHIMSHAM!"
No more beets!

I am going to keep on chanting
Till the magic words appear
"ABRA-CADABRA!"
I will find it
Even if this takes all year.

SIX MEN AND THE DINOSAUR

[A Parody* - With apologies to John Godfrey Saxe]

Six foolish men of Foolishstan
    Wagered they could surmise
The nature of a Dinosaur
    With blindfolds on their eyes
That each by observation might
    Thus prove himself most wise

---

* See 'The Blind Men and the Elephant' by John Godfrey Saxe

The first approached the Dinosaur
Excitement in his limp
He felt the broad and sturdy side
And cried, 'I'll be a chimp!
It seems to me the Dinosaur
Is nothing but a BLIMP.'

The second, feeling of the claw,
Cried, 'Ho! No need to look!
So very curved and smooth and sharp!?
It's like an open book.
This wonder of the Dinosaur
Is very much a HOOK.'

The third tackled the Dinosaur
    With cross and cranky slouch
Felt leather hide under his hands
    And said, 'I'll freely vouch
This creature called the Dinosaur
    Is, but, a leather COUCH.'

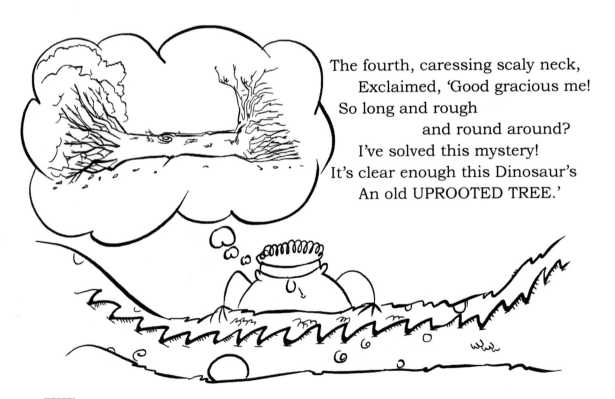

The fourth, caressing scaly neck,
    Exclaimed, 'Good gracious me!
So long and rough
        and round around?
I've solved this mystery!
It's clear enough this Dinosaur's
    An old UPROOTED TREE.'

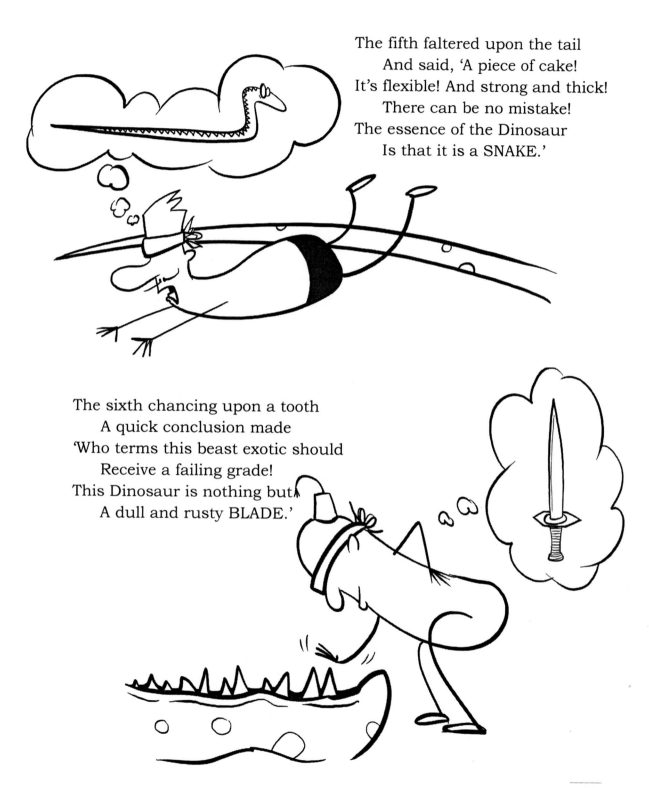

The fifth faltered upon the tail
    And said, 'A piece of cake!
It's flexible! And strong and thick!
    There can be no mistake!
The essence of the Dinosaur
    Is that it is a SNAKE.'

The sixth chancing upon a tooth
    A quick conclusion made
'Who terms this beast exotic should
    Receive a failing grade!
This Dinosaur is nothing but
    A dull and rusty BLADE.'

And while these men of Foolishstan
Disputed wide and long
Each one contending he was right
And all the rest were wrong
The Dinosaur awakened and
Consumed the vocal throng...

CHEWING GUM

Chew, chew, chew, chew
Chew, chew, chew, chew
Chew, chew, chew, chew
   Chewing gum

      I know that you
      Like to chew chew
      Like to chew chew
         Chewing gum

            So I thought that
            As your chum I'd
            Help you chew some
               Chewing gum

                  So I chewed some
                  Just-for-you gum
                  Won't you take some
                    Well-chewed gum?

LIST

Electric Eels
A porcupine
Two leopard seals
A highway sign
A rabid dog
Three rattlesnakes
A hungry hog
Four rusty rakes
A swarm of bees
Five cactus plants
A sack of fleas
Six fire ants
A wolverine
A bed of nails
A cat that's mean
And stingray tails
If you do not
Like getting hurt...

...Don't put these things
Inside your shirt.

THE PANT-EATER OF THE AMAZON

Now all throughout the Amazon
They scoff at feral beasts
Those Jaguars and Piranhas
Don't scare them in the least

But there's one fearsome creature whom
They shun in all the parts
Its name alone is sufficient
To terrorize brave hearts

When told that it's a-prowling, all
The men will flee in fright
The moms hush all the children and
They lock the doors at night

They know that when you face it you
Can seethe and fume and rant
But you can't stop the Pant-Eater
From slurping up your pants!

LET'S MAKE STONE SOUP

Start with water. Drop a stone in.
Look for things that can be thrown in.
Got a craving that you favor?
Don't be shy - let's add that flavor!
What's this? Pungent onion slices?
Paprika and fiery spices?
Hot Tabasco! ... By the pitcher??
Horseradish to make it richer...?
You like peppers? Jalapenos?
Serranos and Habaneros...?
Cayenne Pepper? And Pimento...?
And some piquant condiment-o!!?
Soup is ready. Have a bite now.
Me? I've lost my appetite now.

OVERSLEPT

I overslept this morning
And missed my bus to school
I overslept through breakfast
And missed my daily gruel

I overslept past lunchtime
And through the afternoon
I overslept past dinner
And all the way through June

I overslept through Autumn
Through seasons old and new
I overslept my teen years
And past my twenties too

I've overslept for decades
And now I'm going to scream
What if I wake and find out...

...I wasn't in a dream!

OGRE'S MEAL

(a.k.a. The Toad Not Taken)

[A Parody* - With Apologies to Robert Frost]

Two toads emerged in a yellow wood
And sorry I could not gobble both
And be one gobbler, long I stood
And looked in one as far as I could
And smelled it's scent in the undergrowth

Then took the other, as just as scowled
And having perhaps the better claim
Because it was warty and smelled more foul
Though as for that the passing fowl
Had fouled them really about the same

And both that morning equally lay
In leaves no step had trodden black
Oh, I kept the first for another day
Yet knowing how way leads on to way
I doubted if I should ever come back

I shall be telling this with a cuss
Somewhere ages and ages hence:
Two toads emerged in a wood, and thus -
I took the one more odorous
And that has made all the flatulence.

---

* See 'The Road Not Taken' by Robert Frost

THE COUNTENANCE OF HUMPTY DUMPTY

As Humpty Dumpty, on the wall,
Sat in a cheerless slump
A passerby assumed the worst
And yelled, *HE'S GOING TO JUMP!*

An anxious crowd assembled and
Begged Humpty change his mind
The King's Men and their Horses came
(The Press shadowed behind)

They cordoned off the boulevard
Unfurled a safety net
A nervous chatter filled the night,
The tension, thick as sweat

Then Humpty shuffled in his spot
(The crowd shook with unease)
This isn't what you think, he said
I came here ... for the breeze

You see, I haven't smiled in years
My countenance is skewed
I thought a dose of fresh air might
Invigorate my mood

For mirth lends me no company
I'm always feeling grim
And in my quest to lighten up
I sat here on a whim

But as he spoke he lost his poise
And toppled off the top
And treaded wind with flailing limbs
Down, down the few-foot drop

A solemn silence hushed the street.
All stared in stunned dismay.
Poor Humpty missed the safety net
(What more was left to say?)

The coroner, to close, declared
(As medics cleared the pile)
Humpty, our friend, is gone but look –
At last, he's cracked a smile.

I TRIED TO CLONE A DINOSAUR

I tried to clone a Dinosaur
   From old amber-encrusted drones
But I could not produce much more
   Than half-grown bits of skin and bones

And so I built a Time Machine
   To head back to Jurassic days
To view first-hand all those unseen
   Dinosaurs of the yesterdays

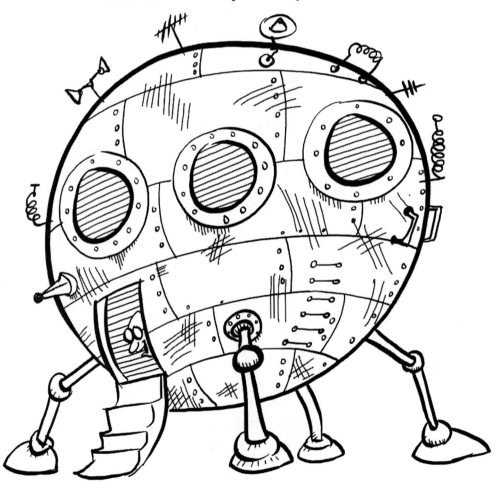

And I came back from this fine trip
Only to find, to my dismay,
Some Dinosaurs stowed on my ship
And breeding in the cargo bay

They looked at me with hungry eyes
I zapped them with my Shrinking Ray
But now that they were all pint-sized
They slipped through cracks and ran away

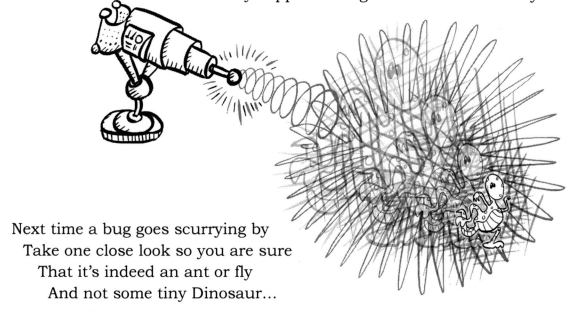

Next time a bug goes scurrying by
Take one close look so you are sure
That it's indeed an ant or fly
And not some tiny Dinosaur...

MOCKTOPUS: A NONSENSE POEM

Once I swam within the ocean,
  Lulled by gentle lapping motion,
    When I suddenly saw something –
    Quaint and curious as can be!
I felt chills within my liver;
  Goosebumps set me all aquiver;
    Could not help but shiver, shiver –
    Shiver in the cold, cold sea!
The sense of dread within my head
    Etched into my memory -
A Mocktopus was mocking me!

Tentacles aflame in color!
  Puckered suckers nowhere duller!
    It was sparing no expense in
      Miming out a parody
With each synchronized contraction,
  How it lampooned my each action
    A bizarre sideshow attraction
      For the natives of the sea!
And with no shame these creatures came
    Adding to my misery;
The Mocktopus was mocking me!

Grudgingly now I must tell you
  Oh, so well it did excel too
    Had I but not my perspective,
      I too might have shared the glee
But I had to keep my focus
  Focused on not being the locus
    Of this mocking hocus-pocus
      In the middle of the sea
So I hurried – hurried, scurried –
    From that scene of mockery;
The Mocktopus was mocking me!

If only that very morning,
  I had not ignored the warning,
    There's a chance I might have skirted
      Facing this ignominy
Now my reputation's tainted;
  Every soul is well-acquainted
    With the tale of how it painted
      Such a spoof of me at sea
How it shamed me – and ill-famed me
    With its mocking mastery;
The Mocktopus was mocking me!

BANG
BLRRRRRR
BANG
WHEEEEEEEEEEEEE
CHIP CHIP
RAT-A-TAT
-A-TAT
HISSSSSSS
BIIIIIIIIIIIIu

BANG
BANG
BANG
BANG

RAT-A-TAT
-A-TAT-
-A-TAT-
-A-TAT-

FORTY WINKS

I'd love to take a little nap –
  (Just forty winks or so)
But noise in this construction zone
  is hampering my flow
The hammer's curt staccato tin-
  tinnabulates my ear
The drill's insistent counterpoint
  keeps stabbing through my cheer
The motor's surly grumbles send
  dissonance up my core
The chisel chip-chip-chips away
  what's left of my rapport
The scraping, pouring, polishing!
  The blare and racket stun!
I guess I won't be napping till
  my dental work is done... :(

BANG

HISSSSSSS
CHIP
CHIP
CHIP
CHIP
WHEEEEEEEEEEEE
BANG BANG

POUND
POUND
POUND
POUND

OMINOUS SIGN

I was born in the grip of an ominous sign
That has tattooed my life with its evil design
It's a fate worse as any that fate can consign
It's a bane to be weathered till stars realign
I have traveled the world with this burden of mine
I have sought out the wise in the rarest of shrines
Though they poked at my toes and they prodded my spine
They had nothing to offer to curb my decline
So from six in the morning to past when I dine
I must go right on living as if it's all fine
But I know, in my heart, it's a matter of time
When my curse reappears and ensures it assigns
Me to wait, yet again, in the slow-moving line
In the slow-moving line, in the slow-moving line
Wherever men queue up to await or combine
That's where I'll be standing, in the slow-moving line...

ROWBOAT FULL OF ROBOTS

There's a rowboat full of robots
Clanking, cranking up the stream
They're a mechanistic marvel
Rowing, rowing as a team

All their gears are spinning, spinning
Eyes a-glowing, flashing bright
Hissing, whirring, beeping, bleeping
Gleaming, gleaming in the light

No expression on their faces
They've a steady, stoic stare
Focused, focused on their mission
Rowing, rowing to somewhere

As their oars go splashing, splashing
Water splatters near and far
I can't help but wonder, wonder
Just how water-proof they are?

(Every robot knows as much that
Water is their biggest threat)
Oops! Their boat is leaking, leaking!
Now they're soaked and sopping wet!

Jerky motion, much commotion
Flailing, bailing with a pail
Metal screeching, grinding, squealing
Circuits frizzle, frazzle, fail

Suddenly, it's very quiet.
(Just a puff or two of steam)
And a rowboat full of robots
Drifting, drifting down the stream

Leaky rowboat, rusting robots
Drifting slowly down the stream...

FOR SALE

For weeks and weeks I've waited here
Hoping a buyer will appear
Are you the one who'll see my deal
Is quite a super-duper steal?

This thing I'm selling isn't new
But I know it's perfect for you!
It's weather-proof! It's oven-safe!
It always fits and never chafes!

I've stored it safely every night!
I've aired it when the sun was bright!
It's washable! And odor-free!
And hundred percent guaranteed!

It never catches germs or bugs!
It's lovable and welcomes hugs!
It's loyal and stays by your side!
And it will be your joy and pride!

Why sell it then? I'm glad you asked!
My dad has set me to this task -
He said I have to sell the stuff
That I am not using enough!

MIDNIGHT HOUR

Well past Fall and shy of Winter
Somewhere, in there, in between
On a night of chills and shadows
Swills the night of Halloween

That's when Ghouls and Ghosts and Goblins
Witches and their Wraiths convene
Riotously overdosed on
Phantasmagoric caffeine

As the midnight hour approaches
As the shivers grow unseen
Supernatural commotion
Germinates an eerie scene

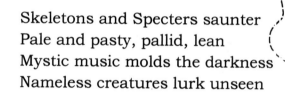

Skeletons and Specters saunter
Pale and pasty, pallid, lean
Mystic music molds the darkness
Nameless creatures lurk unseen

Phantoms float and fade and flicker
Poltergeists cavort, careen
Apparitions shimmer, glimmer
Shrouded in a hazy sheen

Then, at midnight, all goes quiet.
Nothing stirs in wood or green.
Halloween's hijinks seem over
Life is, once more, safe, serene.

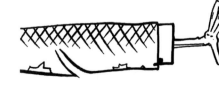 Or is it!? ..... Trick or treat!?

THREE WISHES

As I was going to the fair
I met a most peculiar tramp
He tried to trade my cow for beans
I settled for his magic lamp

My mum got mad, and so she threw
My magic lamp out of the door
Next morning I woke up to find
A genie floating on my floor

COMMAND THY WISH, the genie roared
My first wish was, "A Pot of Gold!"
That genie could not hear too well
He conjured me a pot of *MOLD*

"Not MOLD!" I hollered "Bring me GOLD!"
"Shiny! Shimmering! Lustrous! GOLD!"
But hard of hearing that he was
That Genie plagued me with a *COLD*

YOU'RE SOMEWHAT STRANGE, the genie mused
FOR WHO DESIRES COLDS OR MOLD?
I seethed (and sneezed) and sneezed (and seethed)
"It's GOLD, you dummy! Bring me GOLD!"

They say be careful what you wish
And I can tell you this is true
What made me think the third time round
Would be unlike the other two?

Oh, how I hate that Genie so!
I never got my pot of gold
I was, this morn, a lad of twelve
And now I stand a hundred *OLD*...

FIRST TIME PLAYING BASKETBALL

Yes, we started basketball but
It's not going well at all
Anything we try to do, we
Do it poorly with this ball

We can hardly lift it up and
We can barely run or swoop
We can't dribble, bounce or pass it
No luck shooting through the hoop!

Seems to us our strength is lacking!
Seems to us this game is hard!
Won't you buy our basketball so
We can switch to playing cards?

ANTS

Well, we were messy eaters
We littered night and day
One day the ants found all our crumbs
And made us rue our ways

At first they came in trickles
That quickly swelled to streams
And then they swept in like a flood
That poured in through the seams

Our mum confessed excitement:
"*They're cleaning up the floor!*"
But once the floor was spic-and-span
Those ants marauded more

They raided through our kitchen
They scoured our cupboards bare
They took the cookies, beans, and grains
The apples, plums, and pears

They carried off our sugar
Absconded with our tea
And when they'd taken all our food
They took our new TV

They made off with our sofa
They carted off our bed
The furniture soon disappeared
As did our garden shed

And when the house was empty
The ants ended their spree
But I'm-a-left a-wondering
Where are they taking me?

CURSES: A Villain-elle

I scheme and plot and plan in vain.
Once more I gnash my teeth and sigh:
And curses, I've been foiled again!

My dream is simple, sweet and plain
To rule this world from sea to sky
I scheme and plot and plan (in vain!)

What use my I.Q., my big brain
When fate heckles and pokes my eye
And curses! - *I've been foiled again!*

My death-star, robots, spider-rain,
My dino-clones .... all gone, while I,
I scheme and plot and plan in vain

For no soon have I made some gain
When up pops up some super-guy
- And curses, I've been foiled again!

I'll NEVER give up my campaign
One day I'll win and no more cry:
I scheme and plot and plan in vain,
And curses, I've been foiled again!

FAREWELL

You've reached the end –
Farewell, my friend!
My words are done –
Hope you had fun! :-)

PSSST! HEY, KIDS! GUESS WHAT!?! Did you know you can use this fabulous book as a COLORING BOOK too! Just grab your crayons/pencils/pens and start coloring in all the pictures in this book (or draw your own in the blank spaces)! Then, when you're done, and this book is *fully ruined*, I mean *colored in*, ask a nice grown-up if they will buy you another copy so you can enjoy coloring it all over again. Repeat for endless fun! (Although no, that doesn't mean you're ever going to get your ear back from page 2).

ABOUT
THE AUTHOR

Vikram Madan
is a poet, artist, engineer,
and award-winning cartoonist
who was born and raised in New
Delhi, India and now lives near Seattle,
WA. Back in his elementary school days,
Vikram would often get into trouble for
doodling and rhyming all over his school
books. Imagine his delight in being able
to produce an entire book full of doodles
and rhymes - without getting into any
trouble whatsoever! When he's not
creating stuff, Vikram is usually
out and about trying very
hard to get his hands
on a bubble...

Visit his poetry blog at
http://www.1000Poems.com.

Index of Poems